# A Decade of Serial Killers

# 1950s

# The Most Evil Serial Killers of the 1950s

## Jack Smith

*Warning*
**Throughout the book, there are some descriptions of murders and crime scenes that some people might find disturbing. There might be also some language used by people involved in the murders that may not be appropriate.**

*Note*
Words in italic are quoted words from verbatim and have been reproduced as is, including any grammatical errors and misspelled words.

*ISBN: 9798634272597*

*Printed in the United States*

MAPLEWOOD
— PUBLISHING —

# Contents

# The Good Old Days?

The decade of the 1950s has long been considered the quintessence of the Good Old Days. This designation, of course, is quite inaccurate for many reasons. After all, it was during the 1950s that the world first faced the threat of nuclear annihilation—and due to the tensions of the Cold War, it was not exactly a far-fetched threat. And while it was a relatively prosperous time, that prosperity was not entirely equal. It often depended on what color and what gender you were—the fifties, remember, was before both the civil rights movement and the women's liberation movement really picked up steam.

Serial killers, though, were one group who didn't discriminate. Their ravages cut across all backgrounds and segments of society. And while we've repressed our collective memory of their wanton brutality, all those bebopping jukeboxes and dancing bobbysoxers belie a darker underbelly that existed during this decade. While the 1950s may have been the Good Old Days for some, they were a real nightmare to those unfortunate to cross paths with any of the murderous monsters mentioned in this book.

# Harvey Glatman
# The Cameraman Killer

Harvey Glatman was born in a rough Bronx neighborhood in New York on December 10, 1927, to Ophelia and Albert Glatman. However, his family soon moved out west to try their luck in Colorado. The move was partially out of financial necessity and partly due to persecution. The Glatmans were Jews, and after the stock market crash of 1929, anti-Semitism in New York increased sharply.

Harvey showed some rather disturbing traits and behaviors from a rather young age. When he was just a toddler, his mother caught him wrapping a "string around his penis" and placing the "loose end in a drawer" before "lean[ing] back against the string." Ophelia was horrified, as any mother would be, but she tried to put it out of her mind, hoping that it was just innocent curiosity and not an indication of any untoward behavior to come. He was just a child, after all—surely he didn't know what he was doing?

Unfortunately, this was just the beginning of little Harvey's aberrations. When he was 12, his parents discovered that he was into "autoerotic asphyxiation"—the practice of strangling oneself for sexual satisfaction. Harvey was apparently having the time of his life going up to the attic and tying a rope around his neck. When they'd told him to keep himself occupied on long boring days, they'd never imagined he would choose such a bizarre form of entertainment! This time, Albert and Ophelia didn't ignore the incident; they dialed up the family doctor to schedule an immediate appointment. Now, though, it was the doctor who shrugged it off, simply telling them that Harvey would "outgrow it."

And for a time, it seemed that he had. He finished elementary school on schedule and proved himself to be a good student in middle school. He got good grades in reading and math, and his official record on aptitude tests noted his vocabulary as "excellent." Harvey started high school in 1942, just as World War II was beginning to heat up, and continued to get high marks, mostly A's and B's. He was also quite busy outside of school, joining the Boy Scouts, running track, playing in a band, and getting a part-time job as an usher. That family doctor they'd consulted had advised Ophelia and Albert to keep little Harvey busy—apparently, they did.

But despite all of his extracurricular activities, Harvey had a decidedly hard time when it came to his romantic life. He was most certainly attracted to the opposite sex, but he just couldn't seem to work up the nerve to speak with members thereof. His overwhelming fear of rejection left him unable to relate to the girls in his class, and the growing pressure of this inadequacy soon prompted him to engage in one extracurricular activity that the doctor most certainly didn't order: He began to scope out houses to break into and rob. Harvey was soon arrested and thrown in jail. His poor mom and dad had to bail him out, after which Albert apparently gave his son a "stern talking to."

Maybe not quite stern enough, though, because this would not be the last time that Harvey ended up on the wrong side of the law. Shortly after his high school graduation, in the summer of 1945, he took his trespasses a step further by pulling a gun on an unsuspecting Norene Laurel. Norene was simply out taking a walk that evening when Harvey came out of nowhere, produced his pistol, and ordered her to follow him to his car. The frightened woman complied, and he drove her to a deserted stretch of road. There he parked and got to work tying up his terrified prey. What happened next is a little unclear. Harvey allegedly confessed to "fondling" Norene, but the police report did not indicate that she was raped as it was commonly understood. But even if Harvey just snuggled up next to his victim and took a nap, if he thought that he could simply snatch a woman off the road and force her to cuddle with him, he had another think coming. Almost immediately after Harvey released her, Norene went to the police—and Harvey went to jail.

In the aftermath, his alarmed parents had another doctor examine their son, and this time instead of saying his behavior was something he would simply grow out of, the doctor came back with a diagnosis of schizophrenia. The exact nature of the symptoms that led to this diagnosis remains unclear. Harvey's behavior was obviously bizarre, and like many schizophrenics, he seemed to have a definite disconnect from reality. But there is no evidence that he heard voices or experienced other hallucinations. Nevertheless, his family figured that this diagnosis would be his best defense, allowing him to plead not guilty by reason of insanity.

But when Harvey appeared in court on November 19, 1945, he went against the advice of his lawyer and pled guilty instead. Due to his cooperation, he was given a light sentence of 1 to 5 years in prison. Harvey Glatman turned 18 in a jail cell—hardly an auspicious start to adulthood—but he was out before his next birthday, serving only one year before he was released in 1946. After his release, at the behest of his parents, he relocated to Yonkers, New York, to try to make a new start. He had learned a new trade in prison: how to repair TV sets. Televisions were just then becoming popular, and the need for knowledgeable repairmen—even those with criminal records—gave Glatman a promising career path.

Unfortunately, however, his proclivity for deviant crime resurfaced just a few weeks into his new gig. One night in August of 1946, he confronted a young couple, Thomas Staro and Doris Thorn, with a toy gun. The fake weapon must have looked realistic enough because the startled boyfriend and girlfriend complied with Glatman's commands. Taking them to a secluded area, he had Thomas kneel on the ground, whereupon he tied his hands and feet together and took about $30 from his wallet. Glatman then turned to Doris, ordered her to stand in front of a tree, and tied her hands around the trunk. Then, as Thomas watched in horror, Glatman began to unbutton his girlfriend's shirt.

This dastardly act enraged Thomas so much that he managed to break the ropes around his wrists. Quickly untying his legs, he rushed right at Glatman, nearly knocking him to the ground. Glatman just barely managed to keep his feet, but as soon as he recovered his balance, he dropped his fake gun, pulled out a real knife, and began slashing at Thomas. Thomas was stabbed a couple of times as he struggled to grab hold of the wiry Glatman, and after he began losing a considerable amount of blood, he had to back off. Glatman was certainly not up for a fight, however, and as soon as he was able to get away, he took off running. After freeing Doris, the bloodied Thomas took her to the police station to report what had happened to them and give a physical description of their attacker.

Knowing that the local cops were now looking for a man matching his description, Glatman moved upstate to Albany shortly thereafter. Here he plied his craft of TV repairman by day and deviant criminal by night. His next victim was a woman named Florence Harden, whom he confronted in the middle of the street with his fake gun. He lifted $28 from her purse before attempting to tie her hands together. Florence wasn't going to go down without a fight, though, and while Glatman was preoccupied with his knots, she abruptly shoved him back and began screaming for help. Her cries were enough to send a scared Glatman running away down the street.

He was more frustrated than frightened, however, and he decided to try his luck again the very next night. This time he confronted two women who were walking together—but quickly realized that he had bitten off more than he could chew by having two women to deal with at the same time. Not even trying to tie them up, he settled for taking their money before hightailing it out of there.

He had even worse luck when he tried the same trick a few days later. Alerted to the previous two incidents, police were staking out the area, on the lookout for a man fitting Glatman's description. They caught him in the act of confronting yet another woman, arrested him, and found a fake gun, a knife, and rope on his person. The 19-year-old Glatman was quickly convicted and sentenced to 5 to 10 years in prison. This time around he served most of that sentence, remaining behind bars until 1957.

Upon his release, Glatman traveled over to Los Angeles, California, and it was here that this serial killer's true crime spree would begin. Glatman once again went to work as a TV repairman, but when he wasn't repairing televisions, he was most likely hanging out at the so-called "photography clubs" located in the seedier sections of town. These notorious dens of iniquity allowed patrons to take snapshots as women posed nude for them. More often than not, the women who agreed to do this kind of work were wannabe actresses seeking to get to the next level. Glatman figured this out soon enough and decided to use this angle to exploit his prey.

He first tried what would become his signature ploy on an aspiring actress named Judy Dull. Posing as a publicity agent, Glatman told Judy that he could get her a job posing for a detective magazine. Desperate for the opportunity, Judy followed Glatman back to his apartment for an impromptu photo shoot. Upon their arrival, Glatman informed Judy that she was to play a victim for one of the stories in the magazine—a veritable damsel in distress. The role would require her to be bound and gagged, and Glatman stressed that she needed to appear "convincingly frightened" as if "she was about to be raped."

Judy played her part to the best of her ability, writhing in an imitation of fear and pulling against the ropes that bound her as Glatman snapped photo after photo. But just several minutes into the shoot, things took a darker turn and the fake fear became real. Glatman stopped taking pictures and pulled out his gun. He then cut the ropes and ordered the bewildered Judy to take her clothes off. He then proceeded to sexually assault her several times over the next few hours.

When he eventually got bored with his victim, Glatman had her get dressed again and took her to his car. They drove out to a remote stretch of desert, where Glatman once again assaulted Judy before strangling her to death. After taking a few snapshots of her corpse, positioned in grisly poses, he dumped her body out in the open and took off.

Having finally managed to pull off a successful assault, Glatman decided that murder was the way to go. His next victim was a 24-year-old divorcee named Shirley Ann Bridgeford who had placed a personal ad in the local newspaper. Shirley was just looking for a date, a nice young man who would show her around town and ease her loneliness. What she got when Harvey Glatman answered her ad was altogether more horrible.

Shirley agreed to meet Glatman at her house, and the short, skinny guy who showed up at her door seemed perfectly friendly and non-threatening. So when he asked if she wanted to get in his car and go for a ride, she didn't hesitate to say yes. The night started out innocently enough, and the two got along so well that they eventually parked at a lover's lane to talk and make out.

You might think that for Glatman, who had had such a hard time associating with women in the past, this would have seemed like a dream come true. Sadly, he was so twisted by this point that he couldn't simply enjoy going on a date like a normal guy. And he couldn't take "no" for an answer, either. When Shirley began to resist some of his more aggressive advances, Glatman pulled out a gun, told her to "shut up," and ordered her into the back of the car. There he sexually assaulted his terrified hostage and forced her to pose for some photographs before strangling her to death.

Glatman followed up this grisly crime by luring a woman named Ruth Mercado into his clutches. Like Shirley Ann Bridgeford, he met her through the personal ads, and like Judy Dull, she was an aspiring model. Glatman dialed up the number in the listing and told Ruth that he was a photographer and would be interested in doing a photoshoot with her for a magazine.

Ruth, thrilled at the opportunity, invited him to come over to her apartment. But as soon as Glatman stepped inside, he pulled a gun on her and began ordering her around. In short order, he had herded her into her bedroom and tied her up. As she looked on in terror, whimpering in her bonds, he then ransacked her dresser and stole about $25 in cash. Glatman then told Ruth that he was going to untie her and that if she "cooperated" she wasn't going to get hurt. He raped her several times before having her get dressed again and tying her hands behind her back. Placing a big coat over her shoulders to hide that fact, he led her to his vehicle parked outside and the two drove off in the darkness. When they arrived at a sufficiently isolated locale, Glatman's grisly photoshoot truly began. He ordered Ruth into a succession of perverse poses as he snapped picture after picture. She did everything that he asked, yet he still strangled her to death when he ran out of film.

Glatman's own time ran out soon afterward when he tried the same trick on a woman named Lorraine Vigil. During the car ride, however, Lorraine became aware that things were not all they seemed to be and began to struggle with Glatman. He pulled over to the side of the road and pulled a gun on her, but she wouldn't back down. A fight ensued, and Lorraine managed to tumble out of the car. As luck would have it, a motorcycle-mounted member of the California Highway Patrol just happened to be passing by at that very moment. Seeing the commotion, the policeman screeched to a stop and rushed over and subdued Glatman.

Once again caught red-handed, Glatman readily admitted to his crimes and fully cooperated with the investigation. Nevertheless, he was given a death sentence—and he didn't seem to mind. When the sentence was handed down, Glatman was overheard to say, "It's better this way." Glatman was duly sent to the gas chamber on September 18, 1959.

# Charlie Starkweather
# Gets the Chair

He was born in Lincoln, Nebraska, to Guy and Helen Starkweather. Charlie Starkweather was one of seven children who grew up in the often-impoverished family. His father was a carpenter by trade, but frequent illness often prevented him from working. Helen, a waitress, thus served as the primary breadwinner.

Charlie struggled from the start. Due to a bad lisp and a deformity that caused his legs to be bent, he was routinely ridiculed by his classmates—some of whom would even follow him home to continue their merciless taunts. The mockery only ended when Charlie learned to fight back. To turn the tables on the bullies, he became a bit of a bully himself and began to throw his weight around against anyone who even slightly agitated him. By the time he was 18 he had already dropped out of high school, and his future looked bleak as he struggled to eke out his existence through one dead-end job after another.

The only bright spot in his life was the girl he was seeing—Caril Ann Fugate, whom he had met through his friend Bob Von Busch, who was dating Caril's elder sister, Barb. Caril was just 14, but despite the age gap, her circle of friends generally accepted her relationship with Charlie Starkweather. It was really only her stepfather Marion who disapproved. He did indeed think that Starkweather was too old for the girl, but not only that, he sensed that there was something just not right about the guy. He couldn't quite say why—he just had a hunch—and he had no idea how right he really was.

To be closer to his new flame, Starkweather got a job at a Western Union Newspaper warehouse, which was near the junior high school that Caril attended. The end of Starkweather's shift coincided with Caril's dismissal time, and the two would often meet up with each other then. Most of their dates were pretty mundane, dinner-and-a-movie sort of engagements. But on some occasions, Starkweather would take Caril on hunting trips out in the country. Caril would come to find that Starkweather was a pretty good shot.

Besides hunting, Starkweather would also take Fugate down the back roads and try to teach her how to drive. But this practice ended in disaster when the underage girl ended up wrecking the vehicle in a crash with another motorist. Caril stayed on the scene and spoke with police, but refused to give her phone number when asked. Amazingly, the police did not press her any further; it seems that in the less regulated days of the 1950s, such matters weren't pursued very vigorously.

Caril walked home after the accident, leaving the car right where it was. On her way, though, she was spotted by Bob Von Busch, her sister's boyfriend. When the story came out, Starkweather's dad, as the registered owner of the car, had to pay the damages. This created an enormous rift between Guy and Charlie Starkweather and led to Guy kicking Charlie out of the house.

He wasn't homeless—his friend Bob and Caril's sister Barb, who had just gotten married, allowed him to move in with them—but his unstable situation seemed to send him into a downward spiral. Leaving the warehouse, he got a minimum-wage job as a garbage man and nursed his anger and animosity with grandiose fantasies of robbing banks and going out in a blaze of glory. The only other constant on his mind was Caril, and his thoughts of her were plagued by anxiety because he knew that her parents a) didn't like him—and b) had the power to end their relationship at any time. He couldn't have that, and he, therefore, began to consider acting against them.

In the end, though, it was one random event that set off the coming conflagration. On the night of November 30, 1957, Starkweather was hanging around a neighborhood gas station, as he frequently did when he had nowhere else to go. He could be found there at all hours of the day, often not buying anything, just loitering about and trying to bum cigarettes and soda. On this particular night, he was trying to get the 21-year-old cashier, Robert Colvert, to sell him a stuffed animal on credit. Robert refused, which enraged Starkweather so much that he kept coming back throughout his shift just to harass him. On his final visit, Starkweather pulled a gun on Robert, robbed him, and then forced him to drive to an isolated location, where he shot him and left him for dead—which in fact he was, the first of Starkweather's many victims.

Immediately after the slaying, Starkweather went to a local shop to buy himself some new clothes. He asked the store's owner, Katherine Kamp, if he could "pay with change." She thought he wanted to pay with dollar bills and maybe a few quarters, but to her surprise, he proceeded to sort through a whole pile of pocket change—all of the nickels and dimes that he had cleaned out of the gas station's cash register. This raised Katherine's suspicions, but with no evidence of any wrongdoing, she let it go and sold Starkweather the clothes. But when she turned on the news that very afternoon to hear of a gas station robbery and murder that had taken place the previous night, she remembered the strange young man with pockets full of an inordinate amount of coins and dialed up the police.

Starkweather, meanwhile, was causing his girlfriend Caril increasing concern. He had been acting very odd lately, talking about strange things that didn't seem to make any sense. He would often ramble about wanting to move to Texas, and about how they would both become rich. He never elaborated much on just how these riches would be achieved; he simply told her that all she had to do was follow him and they would have it made.

Caril may have been young, but she wasn't stupid. She knew that the things he was saying didn't add up. And his possessiveness troubled her just as much as his incoherence. Starkweather had always been a touch controlling, but he had suddenly clamped down hard on all of her actions. He would grill her every single day about what she did when he wasn't around, and most especially about what boys she had talked to while she was in class.

His talk of moving to Texas frightened her the most because no matter how crazy his reasons were, she knew that he really did want to quit his job and skip town. Caril certainly wasn't ready for that. She wanted to finish school and become a nurse someday. Throwing all that away was the last thing on her young mind.

Things came to a head-on January 19, 1958, when Starkweather came to Caril's house and began his usual grumpy routine of accusing her of talking to other guys. Caril was tired of it and finally told him, "If you're going to be in such a bad mood, just get out and go home." Starkweather resisted until she finally cried out in exasperation, "I want you to get out and not come back anymore. I don't want to see you ever again!" Her mother then stepped into the fray and sternly informed Starkweather that he needed to go home because he was "upsetting Caril."

Starkweather left—but only to plot his revenge. When he returned to the Fugate residence, it wasn't for a friendly visit, it was to assassinate those he felt were keeping him from the girl he loved. In a fit of murderous rage, Starkweather ambushed the family, killing Caril's mother and stepfather as well as her 2-year-old sister.

Shortly thereafter, Caril came home from school to find Starkweather and the carnage he had unleashed waiting for her. Upon walking through the front door, she was confronted by Starkweather with his rifle aimed right at her. Starkweather shouted, "Sit down!" but the terrified Caril froze in place and Starkweather ended up knocking her down into a nearby rocking chair. Finally getting her bearings and growing defiant, Caril jumped right up and shouted, "Charlie, put down that gun and stop acting so silly!" Starkweather simply knocked her back into the chair again. Caril, becoming upset, stood up for a second time, but this time Starkweather struck her right across the face. She collapsed into the chair and started sobbing.

While Caril cried her eyes out, Starkweather began pacing around and rambling about how "something had happened" to her mother, stepfather, and little sister Betty Jean. He didn't tell her what he had done, though. Instead, he made up an outrageous story that he was involved with a gang of bank robbers and her family had been taken hostage "because they knew too much." In reality, Starkweather had concealed the dead bodies of Caril's family members behind the house.

As an agitated Starkweather continued to pace the floor and ramble his nonsense, Caril finally cried out, "I don't believe a word you're saying, Charlie. You're crazy!"

Starkweather's disturbing response pretty much proved her point as he narrowed his eyes and declared, "If you don't shut up and do everything I tell you, they're dead, you hear? I'll make one phone call and they'll be dead, and it will be your fault. And don't ever, ever call me crazy again or I will kill them!"

As frightened as she was, Caril didn't believe for a minute that what Starkweather was telling her was true. He was in league with bank robbers who had taken her parents hostage? That was absurd. But as she glanced outside to see her stepdad's car in the driveway, and realized that her mom was nowhere to be seen, she came to realize that something had indeed happened to her family. Where were they?

Feeling completely distressed, Caril asked if she could go to the kitchen to make herself a cup of coffee. After she drank it, Starkweather ordered her to change out of her school clothes and into a shirt and jeans. She complied, then sat down on the sofa and once again tried to get Starkweather to tell her what had become of her family. But all he would say was, "If you do everything I tell you to, you can see them later. If you don't, they'll get hurt, and it will be your fault."

Caril, bewildered by the Twilight Zone world she had fallen into, tried to reason with him. "My fault? Charlie, please, this whole thing is so fantastic, I just can't believe…"

Starkweather interrupted her in mid-sentence by tossing his gun at her and shouting, "You don't believe me? Then shoot me! Go ahead. Just shoot me!"

Caril cried out, "Cut it out, Charlie! I'm not shooting you. Why are you acting this way? Why are you acting so crazy? Quit acting so crazy!"

This only infuriated Starkweather even more, however, and he screamed, "Shut the hell up! And didn't I tell you don't ever call me crazy!"

Caril would spend the rest of the night being held hostage and listening to Starkweather rant and rave about all manner of nonsense—none of it true. Her family was not being held hostage by any gang. They were already dead—slain by Starkweather himself. He had killed her mother and stepfather and had even choked her two-year-old sister, Betty Jean, to death. He had discarded their bodies in the backyard of her house. He knew that she would never see them again, but nevertheless, he stuck to his deranged story, telling Caril that her family was being held hostage somewhere and that she had to follow his orders or her parents and little sister would get hurt.

Thus coerced, Caril reluctantly followed Starkweather out of her parents' house on January 27th to begin a murderous rampage that would last for several days. Their first victim was a 70-year-old man named August Meyer who lived in an isolated farmhouse. When the couple stopped off to visit him, Starkweather killed him and even shot his dog. Then they got back in their car and drove on down the road until their vehicle got stuck in the mud and had to be ditched. As they walked along the road they were picked up by a couple of friendly motorists, Robert Jensen and Carol King. Starkweather pulled a gun on them and made them drive to an isolated storm cellar, where he shot Robert in the head. He then began to sexually assault Carol, but abruptly changed his mind and decided to just kill her instead.

The pair then took Robert Jensen's car to the rich side of town, where they broke into the home of Lauer and Clara Ward. The first person they met inside was the maid, whom Starkweather slew with a knife. He then grabbed hold of the Wards' barking dog and crushed its windpipe with his bare hands. It was Mrs. Ward who came home next. She was ambushed and knifed by Starkweather, although he would later claim that Caril had done the stabbing. Mr. Ward then arrived and was duly shot dead by

Starkweather. The couple then proceeded to ransack the place and load up Lauer's car with the stolen goods before taking off in it.

By this time, the police were following their murderous trail with great interest and had set up a dragnet to capture the culprits. Starkweather knew this and realized that he should switch cars. He saw his chance to do so when he encountered a man named Merle Collison who was sleeping in his vehicle on the side of the road. Which of the couple shot Merle is disputed—Starkweather claimed that it was Caril, but she always maintained that she'd never killed anyone—but at any rate, they gunned him down and fled the scene in his car.

Starkweather, however, had neglected to release the parking brake, and they only got a little way down the road before the car suddenly stalled out. As Starkweather struggled to get it started again, a concerned driver pulled over to render assistance. Starkweather declined the offer of aid by brandishing his weapon at the Good Samaritan—just as a deputy sheriff also rolled up. Caril seized the opportunity to escape and ran toward the deputy shouting, "It's Starkweather! He's going to kill me!" Tossing Caril in the back seat of his cruiser, the deputy then gave chase as Starkweather drove off. After a hail of bullets from the pursuing policeman riddled his car, Starkweather decided to surrender, ending his brief but bloody spate of serial murder.

Starkweather initially told investigators that he had forced Caril to come with him and that she had nothing to do with the crimes. Shortly thereafter, however, he changed his story and started claiming that she was a "willing participant." For her part, Caril consistently maintained that she had been compelled to participate in Starkweather's crime spree against her will. Unfortunately for her, the judge noted that there were several occasions on which she could have escaped and gotten help.

Since she hadn't, he reasoned that she must have been more involved in the crimes than she was letting on. The exact nature of Caril's cooperation, however, still remains a matter of intense debate.

The role that Charlie Starkweather played, of course, is not in dispute. After being interrogated, Starkweather placed his signature on a 213-page confession. He was subsequently found guilty of murder and sentenced to death. He was electrocuted on June 25, 1959. His mind was on his beloved Caril until the end, although not in a very nice way; he was quoted as saying, "She should be sitting on my lap in the electric chair."

Caril wasn't shown a whole lot of sympathy at her own trial. Even though she was just barely a teenager, she was tried as an adult for her part in the murder spree and handed a life sentence. However, the term was ultimately reduced to 17 and a half years and she was paroled in 1976. Determined to live a straight life thenceforth, she moved to Lansing, Michigan, and got a job as a hospital custodian. She eventually married in 2007, staying loyally devoted to her husband Fredrick Clair until his tragic death in a car crash in 2013.

The jury is still out on just how much Caril knew at the time of the murders and how much she was actually involved, but at any rate, she served her time and hasn't been in any legal trouble since.

# Edward Gein
# The Ghoulish Fiend

Even in the dark and twisted world of serial killers, Edward Gein was a strange man whose grotesque exploits would go down as some of the worst. But he didn't start out that way; when he began life on August 27, 1906, he was the pride and joy of his parents, George and Augusta Gein. As much as they loved their son, however, they didn't care too much for each other.

George was a chronic drinker who had a very difficult time holding down a job. He was the living epitome of a jack of all trades, master of none. While Edward was growing up, his dad tried his luck at being a tanner, a carpenter, and even an insurance broker. At one point he bought some property and opened up a grocery store, but this went under in just a couple of years and he had to sell it. That wasn't all bad, though, because the proceeds were enough for the family to buy a small piece of farmland around Plainfield, Wisconsin.

It was here that Edward would perfect his own wicked craft. His existence in Plainfield was a lonely one. His mother Augusta, a very religious woman who had turned her back on the world long ago, made sure he had no friends or social life outside of the home. Rather than hanging out with his classmates, every single day without fail, little Edward came home promptly after school and spent the rest of the day helping out around the house.

By the time Edward reached adolescence, Augusta was the undisputed authority in the home. She repeatedly lectured her sons about how the world was an immoral place full of lust and iniquity. Every evening she would hold Bible study sessions and deliver impromptu sermons which, rather than preaching the love and forgiveness of Jesus Christ, usually featured passages on judgment, wrath, and condemnation. She taught her children that they were "in this world but not of this world." Gein already felt ill at ease with his peers, and after listening to his mother's harangues he came to feel like an outright alien.

And if Augusta was domineering while George was alive, after he abruptly passed from cardiac arrest in April of 1940, she became positively tyrannical. And that wasn't the only problem; without the meager aid that their father had provided, Edward and his brother Henry were forced to start working just to keep the family afloat financially. They did this largely by running errands for their neighbors, and Edward, in particular, became a regular babysitter. One theory is that he related well to children because of his own underdeveloped emotional state—in a sense, he was just a big kid himself. Of course, in light of his later crimes, it's now horrifying to think of him spending any time with youngsters at all!

The Gein brothers carried on like this for the next few years, eking out a hard existence on the farm as best they could. Then, in May of 1944, a brushfire on the farm got out of control. In the chaos, Edward somehow lost track of Henry. He notified the police, and a search party soon found his brother's dead body collapsed in the dirt. Curiously, there was no sign of Henry having been burned by the fire. His clothes were singed, but he was otherwise unharmed by the blaze. However, there were some noticeable bruise marks on his head. This has since led to speculation that Henry may have been Edward's first victim, that perhaps he struck him over the head and killed him. But this theory has never been proven, and medical examiner at the time certainly did not make this determination. On the contrary, he recorded Henry's cause of death as asphyxiation. It seemed entirely possible that Henry had succumbed to smoke inhalation and collapsed, striking his head in the process and causing the bruises, and no one at the time had any reason to suspect otherwise.

With both George and Henry now out of the picture, it was just Edward and Augusta who were left to work the farm. And Augusta didn't last much longer. In 1945 she suffered a massive stroke, suddenly informing her son that she was feeling "faint and sickly" and needed medical attention. Edward promptly loaded her into the car and drove her to the nearby Wild Rose Hospital. By the time they arrived, Augusta was unable to walk on her own power, so she was taken to an examination room in a wheelchair. After it was confirmed that she had sustained a stroke, she was admitted to the hospital in order to stabilize her condition.

Edward made sure to visit her every single day and soon became a permanent fixture at her side. When she was eventually discharged, it was Edward who dutifully brought her home and arranged for her to get her bed rest. He helped in every way he could, taking over all of the duties of the farm and reading his mother her favorite psalms from the Bible when she was able to form enough words to request it. Just as he was getting used to this new situation, though, Augusta suffered another stroke—this time severe enough to finish her off.

It was December of 1945. Edward Gein was 39 years old, single, and with such poor social skills that he scarcely had any hope of ever getting married. The death of his mother left him all alone in a deeply troubled and isolated existence. With nothing else to do, he carried on with his backbreaking work on the farm as best he could.

Those who occasionally encountered him when he ventured out to buy something at the local store or dared to sit down for a drink at the local bar barely noticed any difference. Gein was already considered an oddball—but it was an oddness that everyone in town was quite used to. As such, they didn't perceive him as being any weirder or more troubled than he already had been. He seemed like the same strange guy they had known for years.

Even after bartender Mary Hogan vanished without a trace and Gein joked that she was hanging out at his farm, most just assumed it was an example of Gein's decidedly offbeat humor. Little did they know that in an extremely morbid way, Gein was actually telling the literal truth—as investigators would one day discover when they came upon Mary's mortal remains strung up like slabs of butchered meat on Gein's property.

A few years later, Bernice Worden, the owner of a hardware store, went missing with a trail of blood leading out the store's back door. Attention turned to Gein when it was discovered that he had been her last customer—a fact documented by a receipt for the half-gallon of antifreeze he had purchased just moments before Bernice vanished. When police paid an impromptu visit to Gein's home, they were absolutely shocked at what they found. Rather than hiding his crime, Gein had displayed his atrocities in plain sight, hanging the butchered corpse of Bernice Worden in an extra kitchen located behind the house. She was strung up by her feet, attached to a pulley. Her head had been cut clean off, and her innards had been removed.

After calling for backup, the officers searched the entire home and made a number of grisly discoveries, including decapitated heads and even sheets of skin wrapped around Gein's furniture as a macabre form of decoration. Perhaps most distressing of all was the secret shoebox of butchered vaginas they found under Gein's bed. If Gein had been sexually repressed by his mother's constant condemnation of all things worldly, he had certainly found an extreme way to finally express his urges.

Although Gein was being investigated just for the disappearance of Bernice Warden, the multiple body parts—including the perfectly preserved faces of nine women dried out and mounted on his wall—clearly indicated that his killing spree was much more extensive than that. And he did fit the stereotype of the meek and mild, totally unsuspected serial killer in a truly horrific way. However, Gein himself had another explanation. He confessed to killing both Mary Hogan and Bernice Worden, but he claimed that all the other body parts belonged to women he had dug up from the nearby cemetery. Ever since his mother's death, he said, he had been obsessed with the place and had routinely pillaged fresh graves so that he could butcher his own souvenirs.

It still remains unclear just how many women Gein may have killed, but he is certainly known as one of the most horrific killers of the 1950s all the same. So horrific in fact, that Alfred Hitchcock's famed film *Psycho* features a horrendous killer said to be based on Gein. As terrible as Gein's crimes were, however, he would not go to prison for them. Deemed to be mentally ill, he was sent to live the rest of his life in an insane asylum instead. That he did without further incident, passing away from cancer on July 26, 1984.

Upon his death, he was taken back to the same graveyard his mother was buried in and laid to rest by her side. It was an entirely fitting—yet totally sickening—end.

# Peter Manuel
# The Man Who Talked Too Much

The murderous misfit Peter Manuel was born in New York in 1927. His parents were originally from Britain and had moved to the U.S. shortly beforehand. Things didn't quite work out for the family in America, however. After the 1929 stock market crash, the Great Depression made both work and money scarce, and so in 1932, the Manuels moved back to the British Isles, settling in Birkenshaw, Lanarkshire, in Scotland.

Peter had a rough go of things in Scotland and was allegedly bullied as a child. Wishing to become tough, he ended up hanging out with the wrong crowd, and by the time he was 11 years old, he had already earned a criminal record for busting open an offering box in the sanctuary of a local church. It's bad enough when a kid steals, but when he's depraved enough to steal from a church, it's a pretty clear indication of just how deficient his moral compass actually is!

In fact, it had already been noted that Peter had no conscience whatsoever. One of his teachers would later recall how she found an obscene drawing that Peter had left in the classroom, and just how stone-faced he was when confronted with it. Most boys would have been mortified by such a discovery, but not Peter. He wasn't embarrassed or concerned at all. He basically shrugged his shoulders and said, "Yeah—that's mine. So what?"

In the fall of 1939, the troubled youth started a veritable crime spree. For the rest of that year and well into 1940, he committed instance after instance of "shop breaking and larceny." He was eventually caught and found guilty of breaking and entering, but as he wasn't old enough to go to jail, he was placed in a kind of reform school for troubled youth instead.

The school didn't reform him very much, though, and on March 21, 1946, he was arrested on another 15 charges of breaking and entering. When his father bailed him out, the psychopathic Peter Manuel embarked on yet another crime spree without missing a beat. This time, however, instead of just stealing, he began to assault women he found home alone. He attacked a total of three women during this period. Two of them put up stiff resistance and managed to drive him off; the third was not so lucky and was sexually assaulted. Promptly identified by his latest victims, Manuel was sent to prison for eight years.

He resented it, and upon his release in 1953, he began to think long and hard about just how he would strike back against society. He worked a civil service job by day, but by night he was hatching all manner of murderous schemes.

In 1955, Manuel ran afoul of the law once again when he was accused of sexual assault. However, he was somehow able to convince the jury that the act was consensual, resulting in a verdict of not guilty. But the jurors who allowed him to beat the rap would come to regret it a year later when Manuel turned his peccadilloes into outright, cold-blooded murder.

It was a 19-year-old girl named Ann Knielands who would become his first victim. Manuel cornered her and beat her to death by smashing her skull in with an iron bar. When Ann's battered body turned up, Manuel quickly turned up on police radar due to his criminal record and the fact that he was working at a nearby location. The problem was that he had what seemed like an ironclad alibi: He told the cops that he'd been staying at his parents' house during the time of the slaying—and his father backed up the claim, even though he was well aware that it was a total lie.

A short time later, Manuel did go to jail, but only on an attempted burglary charge for which his dear old dad promptly bailed him out. This allowed him to break into the home of the Watt family on September 17, 1956. Inside he found Marion Watt, her 16-year-old daughter Vivienne, and her sister Margaret Brown. Coldly and ruthlessly, Manuel shot each of them execution-style. Once again he was questioned shortly after the killings, but with no solid evidence against him, he was released.

While still on bail for the burglary charge, Manuel then proceeded with his killing spree. He hailed a cab and killed the driver Sidney Dunn in what amounted to nothing other than a random act of senseless violence. Just a few weeks later, he sexually assaulted and murdered a girl named Isabelle Cooke.

Manuel's final group of victims was the Smart family. Manuel murdered 45-year-old Peter Smart along with his wife and their 10-year-old child. As in the previous family killing, they were all killed execution-style.

This time, however, Manuel was conclusively linked to the crime after he attempted to use cash that had been stolen from the Smart residence—and this time, he apparently knew that the jig was up and readily confessed. He was so eager to describe the events that he was nicknamed "The Man Who Talked Too Much." He was found guilty as charged and executed on July 11, 1958.

# Melvin Rees
# Also Known as the Beast

There isn't too much recorded about the early days of the murderous monster known as Melvin Reese, but by the first few years of the fifties, he was enrolled at the University of Maryland just outside of Washington, D.C. He spent most of his time refining his skills as a jazz musician and was said to be quite talented on the piano, saxophone, and clarinet.

Rees was good enough, in fact, that he decided to drop out of school to play music full time, trading UMD's College Park campus for the bars and nightclubs of downtown D.C. His nights of clubbing were interrupted by serious criminal charges in 1955 when he was accused of trying to force a woman into his vehicle, but the victim eventually dropped the charges and the matter was forgotten. This would not be the end of Rees's delving into deviousness, however—in fact, it was just the beginning.

On June 26, 1957, Margaret Harold just happened to walk right into the crosshairs of this maniac. Margaret and her boyfriend, an army sergeant were parked at a lover's lane when their romantic getaway was interrupted by Melvin Rees. He confronted the couple with a gun and demanded that they "get off of his property." This was patently absurd; they were on a public road, and in any event, Rees did not even own any real estate in the first place. And his next request certainly wasn't a typical property owner's response to trespassers: he demanded that Margaret and her boyfriend give him all their money.

It all sounded pretty ridiculous to Margaret, too, and she indignantly refused to comply. But it turned out that Rees was dead serious. He didn't ask twice; he simply shot her in the head.

Her boyfriend immediately jumped out of the car and ran to get help, leaving Rees alone with the corpse, which disgustingly enough he then proceeded to sexually violate. By the time the police arrived, however, he was long gone.

Rees didn't strike again until January of 1959 when he encountered a family driving down the road and used his car to force them onto the shoulder. Waving his gun, he then ordered them into his car, whereupon he drove them to a remote location and decimated the entire family. A short time later, investigators found his gruesome handiwork. The father, Carroll Jackson, had been shot in the head, and his infant daughter Janet was found underneath him, apparently smothered to death by her own father's corpse. The mother, Mildred, and her five-year-old daughter had both been sexually assaulted before being murdered.

In the aftermath of these slayings, the police received an anonymous tip that local jazz artist Melvin Rees was behind the horrendous crimes. The tipster claimed that Rees had confessed to the murders while high on drugs. The FBI then took a look at Rees' house and found that his saxophone case was full of handwritten recollections penned by Rees himself which related all the gruesome details of the killings.

No one but the culprit could have known such details, so Rees was promptly charged with murder. He was subsequently found guilty and sentenced to death in the electric chair. But at the last minute, the decision was overturned and he ended up getting life in prison instead. He remained behind bars until the day he died.

# Joseph Taborsky
# The Mad Dog Killer

Joseph "Mad Dog" Taborsky, along with his later partner in crime Arthur "the Meatball" Culombe, launched a reign of terror on the East Coast of the United States during the late 1950s. Taborsky himself had a rather long rap sheet stretching back to when he was only five years old and including a string of petty thefts and larcenies throughout his misspent youth.

This early crime spree came to an end when he was thrown behind bars for the 1951 slaying of a man at a Connecticut pub. Up until this point, Joseph's brother Albert had often joined in his misadventures. But in the aftermath of the murder, Albert decided he didn't really want to join Joseph on death row and cut a deal with the prosecution. He accordingly got off with a life sentence, while Joseph did indeed receive the death penalty.

The crafty Joseph wasn't willing to give up quite yet, however, and while awaiting execution he managed to get the attention of the Connecticut Supreme Court, which reviewed his case and decided that Albert was an unreliable witness because he was insane. Albert was, in fact, under wraps at an insane asylum by this point, but it's not clear why that should have rendered his previous testimony invalid. But that's how the court saw it, and when prosecutors attempted to convene a second trial for Joseph, their case simply fell apart without Albert on the witness stand. As astonishing as it may seem, this was all it took to take Joseph Taborsky from death row to freedom.

It wouldn't be long before Taborsky would begin his murderous machinations all over again. The bloodbath began after he hooked up with an old associate of his, Arthur "the Meatball"

33

Culombe. The pair's first rampage occurred on Thanksgiving Day, 1956, when they held up a hotel and a couple of liquor stores. No one died in these crimes, but in every single one of them, the victims were severely beaten—in some instances nearly to death. Since they had complied with the robbers' demands, this was completely unnecessary, wanton violence. The police immediately realized that they had a real vicious character on their hands.

Things only got worse from there. On December 15th, Taborsky and Culombe robbed a man named Nickola Leone who ran a small clothing store in Hartford, Connecticut. This time they didn't just beat him; they shot him in the head. Nikola miraculously survived this wound, but the next victim would not be so lucky. Mad Dog and Meatball proceeded directly to a gas station where they robbed owner Edward Kurpiewski, forced him into the station's restroom, and shot him in the head—this time killing him instantly.

Just then an unfortunate motorist pulled up to get some gas. After being grabbed by the duo and hauled into the station's garage, he was executed as well. Meanwhile, the man's little daughter was sleeping in his car, blissfully unaware that her father's life had just been taken. Thankfully, the girl herself was not harmed and would be later discovered by a bus driver.

Taborsky and Culombe showed no signs of stopping their rampage. On December 21st they held up a local grocery store, brutally pistol-whipping owner Arthur Vinton before loading up on the store's cash. The duo then moved on to rob another liquor store, where they gunned down Samuel Cohn as he stood behind the counter. Next, they invaded a shoe store in New Haven, hauled owner Frank Adinolfi into a back room, and beat him into oblivion. As they were brutalizing Frank, a couple of unwitting customers came into the store. Joseph wasted no time in confronting them. Waving his gun, he ordered them to kneel on the ground and then blew their brains out.

Stories like this should serve as a lesson to anyone who's tempted to believe a crook when he tells them, "Just do what I say and you won't get hurt." Taborsky's victims did everything he asked and were still gunned down for no other reason than to fulfill his blood lust. No one should meekly acquiesce to a maniac like this without putting up a fight!

As the murderous pair continued their rampage across the East Coast, Frank Adinolfi recovered enough to report what he had witnessed to the police. One of the key details was that the man who attacked him wore a size 12 shoe. The keen eyes of this shoe salesman would prove invaluable because there weren't many men who wore such large shoes. When the police looked through their records, they quickly came across the profile of Joseph Taborsky. And when they showed his photo to Frank Adinolfi, he confirmed that this was the man who had robbed him and beaten him within an inch of his life.

Unfortunately, this breakthrough did not arrive soon enough to prevent this serial killer from striking again. On January 16, 1957, Taborsky held up a drugstore in Hartford and shot the owner, John Rosenthal, right through the heart. John's son Henry was downstairs when he heard the gunshot. He came up and caught Taborsky off guard while he was cleaning out the cash register. Seeing the man's gun, Henry tried to make a run for it, but he wasn't quick enough. He was shot dead in front of his father's store as the mad dog killer came barreling out after him, his gun blazing.

The police did catch up with Taborsky shortly thereafter, and although he remained fairly quiet during his interrogation, his partner Meatball Culombe proved to be quite a talker. Just like

Albert Taborsky had done when he'd been ratted out by his own brother years ago, Meatball laid out every detail of the crimes that they had committed—and claimed that Joseph Taborsky was the one behind all of them.

Meatball, although not very bright, wasn't insane, and Taborsky knew he wasn't going to be able to wriggle his way out of this one. He soon decided it was in his best interest to just confess. It didn't save him from the death penalty, though—and Columbe's cooperation didn't save him, either.

Incredibly enough, however, the Supreme Court stepped in once again—not on behalf of Taborsky, but on behalf of Arthur Culombe. The justices determined that the police had "gone too far" during their interrogation of the Meatball and violated his civil rights, and his sentence was accordingly reduced to life in prison.

Joseph Taborsky had run right out of luck, however, and was duly electrocuted on May 17, 1960.

# Leslie Irvin
# The Hoosier Hit Man

Indiana is probably better known for the Indy 500 and cornfields than for crime, but nevertheless, some of America's most prolific killers and crooks have indeed come out of the Hoosier State. From bank robber John Dillinger to more recent serial killers, Indiana has never had a shortage of murder and mayhem.

During the 1950s, a local boy named Leslie Irvin was the one terrorizing his fellow Hoosiers and leaving a bloody trail all over a tri-state area. His first victim was a pregnant 33-year-old named Mary Holland. Mary was behind the counter of her husband's liquor store in Evansville—a town in the southeastern corner of the state—when Irvin walked in and announced a robbery. Her husband had always told her to "play it smart" and give in to the demands of any would-be robber. It wasn't worth losing her life over money, he said. So Mary simply complied with Irvin's demands and handed over everything in the cash register. But Irvin wasn't your normal robber—he was a cold-blooded killer. And even though Mary put up no resistance whatsoever, he gunned her down anyway, seemingly for no other reason than the thrill of the kill. He then dragged the pregnant woman's body to the bathroom and shoved her behind the toilet.

When Mary's husband came to the store later that day, he immediately knew that something wasn't right. There was a half-empty bottle of whiskey on the counter next to the open cash register. He knew that Mary wouldn't leave the cash register open and just take off, and he knew that his pregnant wife would not be drinking a bottle of whiskey! His mind screamed that an intruder had done something to his wife. He began to call frantically for her, but there was no response. Then he saw the trail of blood. Following it to the bathroom, he found the grisly sight of his wife's body wedged behind the toilet. She was wedged in so tight, in fact, that it would take several police officers to pull her out.

In total, the killer had taken about $250—quite a haul for the time. But the detective assigned to the case, Dan Hudson, told the Evansville newspapers the following day that there was no doubt that money wasn't the killer's main motivation. This incident was "a cold-blooded crime." They were dealing with someone who had absolutely no respect for life. And Detective Hudson was right, for this callous slaying was just the beginning of a whole spate of ruthless killings across Indiana and beyond.

The next victim was a gas station attendant named Wesley Kerr who was working the late shift at a Standard Oil off Highway 41. Right around midnight, a gunman stormed into the station and shot Kerr execution-style before cleaning out the cash register. Just like Mary's, Wesley's body was found dumped in the bathroom. It was a cruel end for a family man who was a dedicated husband and father of three kids. Wesley was also a veteran who had lived through both World War II and the Korean War. He had served his country with distinction overseas, only to be gunned down in his own country and left for dead next to a gas station toilet.

The next victim of this madman was a woman named Wilhelmina Sailer who was murdered on March 21, 1955. Slain execution-style just like the rest, she was found in a pool of blood by her little son who had just gotten out of school. Instead of getting a snack and sitting down in front of the TV to watch cartoons like he normally would, this poor child found his mother with half of her head blown off by a gun blast. Wilhelmina's husband John came home just a few minutes after their son, and through his horror, he noted that although his wife's purse had been pilfered through, only a few dollars had been taken. The devastation wrought for such a small amount of money once again showed investigators that in these horrendous crimes, robbery was secondary—the primary motive was the killings themselves.

When this grisly murder hit the news, the public was on the verge of panic. It's a stereotype to say that a community is so safe that people don't lock their doors—but in Evansville back then, a lot of people didn't even *have* locks. In the days to come, however, local hardware stores rapidly sold out of door locks, bolts, and other security equipment.

The killer was already moving on, however, crossing over Indiana's southern border to seek his next batch of victims in Kentucky. Here he besieged the farm of one Goebel Duncan. He caught this rural Henderson County homestead by complete surprise and held the family hostage before killing Goebel and two of his family members. Goebel's wife was shot in the head as well, but miraculously enough, she lived through the ordeal. She would be blind for the rest of her life, though, and when she finally woke up in her hospital bed, her memory was gone—and with it her ability to serve as a witness to the horrendous acts.

But it happened that others had been nearby and were able to fill in some of the details. A group of neighborhood teenagers had been hanging out down the street from the farm and had seen a suspicious man coming and going from the Duncan residence. Coincidentally enough, they had just been discussing the recent slayings and joking about becoming vigilantes to hunt the miscreant down. Just then, they saw the stranger leaving their neighbor's house. Getting his attention, one of the kids called out, "Stop! We're investigators!" Upon hearing this, Irvin hopped in his car and took off, which of course only made him seem all the more suspicious. One of the teens was quick enough to take down his license plate number, and he reported it to the police shortly thereafter.

Just a quick search through police records showed that the Indiana plate had been issued to Leslie Irvin, who had previously served time for a burglary in Indianapolis. His past as a petty criminal was apparently over, though; now he was an all-out serial killer, and as such, he took top priority. Police quickly launched a manhunt to track him down, which they did without too much trouble.

Nor did they have much trouble getting him to confess to the killings. The hard part turned out to be getting him to face justice for them. Just before he was to be transferred to Indiana State Prison, Irvin managed to stage a stunning escape, breaking through several locked doors in the prison and fleeing right out onto the street. From there he just kept running, racing across the country, reaching Los Vegas, then Los Angeles, before finally ending up in San Francisco—crossing an astonishing 2,000 miles in less than a month's time. But while Irvin could certainly run, he couldn't hide, and when he tried to unload some stolen goods at a San Francisco pawnshop, this murderous crook's time on the lam came to an end.

Leslie Irvin stood trial in 1969 and was found guilty as charged. He spent the rest of his life in prison, dying on November 9, 1983.

# Dedan Kimathi
# The Mau Mau Killer

Dedan Kimathi, born in colonial Kenya on October 31st, 1920, grew up to be one of the worst serial killers the world has ever known. Not only was he a serial killer, but he also cobbled together a diabolical band of serial killers, directing them to follow his lead in brutality. In Dedan's case context is everything, however, and as gruesome as the crimes, the motives and circumstances are fairly different from your typical serial murderer.

Despite his debauchery, Dedan was viewed in some parts of Kenya as a revolutionary of sorts, seeking to shake off the British yoke. The British had reigned supreme in Kenya since the 1890s and even after losing the vast majority of their territory in the aftermath of World War Two, the Brits were still desperately clinging to Kenya by the 1950s. This was the colonial backdrop in which Dedan Kimathi grew up.

As an adolescent, Dedan was known to be a good student and made high marks. He was particularly remembered as being an excellent debater and often participated in vigorous debates with other students. The prime topic, of course, was usually a political one, about how Kenya might one day gain independence from the British. As good as a student as he was, during his teenage years he found it difficult to come up with the fees necessary to keep up his attendance.

Without any means to pay for his tuition, he was forced to drop out. During the 1940s, Dedan entered the workforce taking various lowly, menial jobs such as being a janitor, day laborer, and even a dairy farmer. When he wasn't working, Dedan still made use of his interest in debate and politics by joining up with an independence driven organization called the "Kenyan African Union" or just "KAU" for short.

Dedan quickly rose through the ranks of the KAU until he managed to become secretary for his local branch of the organization. Years later when he was arrested for his murder spree, Dedan would claim that he rubbed shoulders with prominent Kenyans, including the future president Jomo Kenyatta. But it was among the militant Muhimu or as it was sometimes known the "Forty Group" that Dedan became the most active.

This wing of the KAU consisted mainly of ex-Kenyan military, political activists, and all-out hoodlums. Anyone who had a beef with society was a part of this disgruntled group. The group soon became known for violent, terrorist styled attacks throughout colonial Kenya. They often burned down farms, conducted assassination, and organized various other random acts of violence. It was amid these violent acts that Dedan Kimathi found himself on the wrong side of the law in the Fall of 1952.

He was taken into custody, suspected to have taken part in a spate of slayings that had killed British settlers as well as a senior Kenyan chief administrator, Nderi Wang Ombe. These crimes sent shockwaves through the colonial regime and led to an all-out crackdown on those believed to have been involved in the violence. It remains unclear just how much Dedan Kimathi was involved in this murderous campaign, and he soon escaped prosecution by bribing a sympathetic guard who allowed him to flee from his prison cell.

Upon his escape, Dedan sought refuge in the vast "Nyandarua forest" where he would continue a guerilla campaign against the colonial government. It was here in the depths of the forest that

Dedan Kimathi would continue to build his following among fellow rabble-rousers and he would come to prominence in the "Mau Mau" movement. Although the British would later label the Mau Mau as a kind of cultish group, that lacked popular support.

It is true, that in some ways, Dedan's group did indeed have the characteristics of a murderous cult. Dedan led his followers by strange dictatorial precepts of his own making, similar to the likes of Charles Manson and his "Manson Family." Dedan believed that he was creating his own functional government of which he would wield absolute authority over.

Like Manson, Dedan also practiced a form of "free love" in the outlaw society he fashioned, but ironically enough, it was only free for Dedan himself to take part in. Dedan had expressly forbidden his male followers from having any "sexual affairs" with the "female fighters" that were under his charge. Yes, the forward-thinking Dedan had plenty of female warriors join his militia, and he wanted to make sure that the men under his charge did not associate with them.

But for Dedan on the other hand, it was a completely different story. He was actually quite prolific in his "sexual affairs" with the female members of his group. So much so, that some described him as having a "harem of lovers" in the forest. Dedan's most famous of these lovers was a woman named Wanjiru Wambogo. She was handpicked by Dedan to be a kind of role model for the other women of the group, and was given the "rank of colonel." Along with being Dedan's loyal colonel, she also happened to give birth to a few of Dedan's children during the years they sojourned in the wilderness.

The struggle against the British would begin to heat up by the mid-1950s, and the Mau Mau began to increase their attacks against the colonial authority. At first, the colonial administration viewed them as nothing more than a mild nuisance, or as one official puts it, they were viewed as nothing more than a bunch of "unruly youths who should return to productive labor and familial obligations."

But these unruly youths would soon strike terror right into the heart of British Kenya. Dedan would direct his followers to kill civilian settlers and colonial officials alike in a crime spree that would leave hundreds of people dead. Not only was the sheer number of dead shocking but also how they died. Many of the victims were chopped into pieces and butchered as if they were nothing more than animals that Dedan and his eager crew had slaughtered.

As was the case when the young son of a tribal chief was cut in half simply because his father refused to join Dedan Kimathi's cause. To punish the family, the innocent child was sliced in two. Dedan and his men are said to have then "drank the blood" of the boy, before tossing the child's blood drained remnants at his mother. The mom was then subsequently murdered as well.

As bad as serial killers and cultish, murderous groups can be, Dedan Kimathi and his band of followers seemed to take wanton acts of cruelty and utter brutality to whole new levels. They certainly used fear, terror, and death as weapons to achieve their revolutionary ideals, and Dedan for his part never appeared ashamed of his actions in the least. For him, it was just a means to an end, and the lives that were lost were simply collateral damage as he pursued his goal.

Dedan Kimathi's control over his band of guerrilla fighters would eventually fall apart, however, and he would get ratted out by one of his former members. Seizing on the valuable intel that this former associate had provided, Dedan was eventually corned in the forest, and captured by local, "tribal police." Dedan would then be tried, sentenced and executed in 1957, putting an end to his reign of terror once and for all.

Although this was the end of Dedan Kimath's life however, it wasn't the end of his story, since his legacy that continues to evolve with time. Because just as the old expression goes, "one man's terrorist is another man's freedom fighter." In 2007, some fifty years after Dedan's execution, Dedan was being openly hailed as a revolutionary hero by the Kenyan government.

The Brits have long since pulled out of their old colonial project, and their successor Kenyan government has since recognized Dedan Kimathi not as a serial killer/terrorist ring leader, but as one of their founding fathers, even placing a statue of Dedan in Kenya's capital. Many in Britain were outraged at the commemoration of Dedan's atrocities, but as of 2020, most in Kenya tend to regard him in a much more benign light.

So just who was Dedan Kimathi? Was he one of the worst serial killers of the 1950s? Or a much-misunderstood fighter for Kenya's liberty and freedom? I suppose with this one—history will have to be the judge.

# Not So Good After All

The 1950s are often looked back upon with great nostalgia. The music, the tail-finned cars, the TV shows, the fast-food joints are all remembered with relish. The decade certainly was a carefree time for many—but little did they know that lurking in the backdrop of these fond memories was a whole cadre of bloodthirsty killers.

The likes of Ed Gein are certainly not what most people think of when they think of the 1950s, but they were part and parcel of the decade nonetheless. This was also the decade that crazed criminals such as Melvin Rees and Leslie Irvin raped, robbed and murdered in cold blood all over the United States.

Yes, we live in uncertain times today—but one might take a strange bit of solace in knowing that the times have always been a little bit uncertain. The grass may look greener on the other side, and the past sometimes seems better than the present, but this is usually only the product of our wishful thinking. Because when we take the time to consider it, the good old days really weren't all that good in the first place.

# Further Readings

Now that we have brought this book to a close, we would like to introduce you to some of the reading and reference material that has helped to make this book possible in the first place. Here you will find wide-ranging material that has served to cover various aspects of the cases. Feel free to go through them all.

## Rope: The Twisted Life and Crimes of Harvey Glatman. Michael Newton

This book, much as the title might describe, goes over the whole twisted narrative that was the life of Harvey Glatman. This book provides a good reference point as to Harvey's motivations as well as a good insight into his family members and the lives of his victims. If you need an in-depth analysis of the sordid tales of this manmade monster, Newton's text certainly provides it.

## The Twelfth Victim: The Innocence of Caril Fugate in the Starkweather Murder Rampage. Linda M. Battisti & John Stevens Berry

This book gives good detail on Charlie Starkweather's life and crimes, but it also shines a bright light on his accomplice/victim, Caril Fugate. There is still much debate concerning just how much of a willing or unwilling accomplice Caril was to Starkweather's rampage, and this book explores the possibilities.

### Deviant: The Shocking True Story of the Original "Psycho". Harold Schechter

This text proved to be a good resource when it came to the life of Edward Gein. It provides details of his childhood, and what possibly motivated him to commit his heinous acts. For anyone wanting to know more about Gein and what drove him to murder, Harold Schecter's book is a valuable resource.

### Peter Manuel, Serial Killer. Hector Macleod and Malcolm McLeod

Here you will find plenty of relevant facts about the life of Peter Manuel. From his childhood to the string of murders he committed, this book provides fairly relevant information.

### American Murder: Criminals, Crimes, and the Media. Mike Mayo

This book is an anthology of crimes of all sorts and provided many additional details on several of the cases presented here.

# Also by Jack Smith

Just click on the book cover to check any of them out.

To visit Jack Smith author's page, please click here

In the Most Evil Serial Killers by Decade series:

Others:

REAL LIFE PSYCHIC DETECTIVES — JACK SMITH

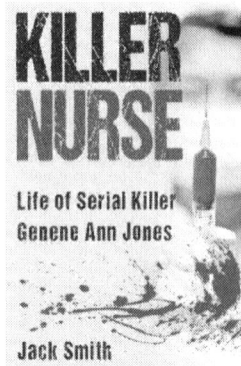
KILLER NURSE — Life of Serial Killer Genene Ann Jones — Jack Smith

THE SCORECARD KILLER — LIFE OF SERIAL KILLER RANDY STEVEN KRAFT — JACK SMITH

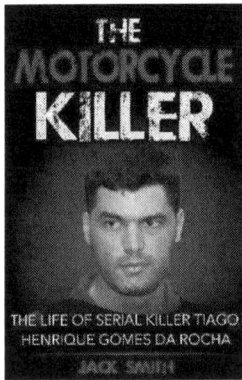
THE MOTORCYCLE KILLER — THE LIFE OF SERIAL KILLER TIAGO HENRIQUE GOMES DA ROCHA — JACK SMITH

THE BUTCHER BAKER — Life of Serial Killer Robert Christian Hansen — Jack Smith

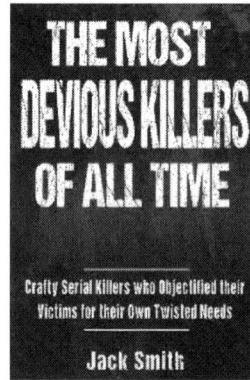
THE MOST DEVIOUS KILLERS OF ALL TIME — Crafty Serial Killers who Objectified their Victims for their Own Twisted Needs — Jack Smith

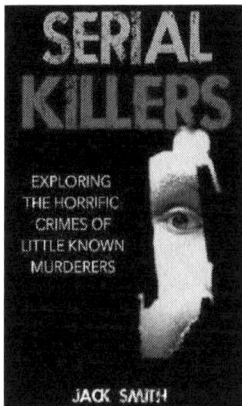
SERIAL KILLERS — EXPLORING THE HORRIFIC CRIMES OF LITTLE KNOWN MURDERERS — JACK SMITH

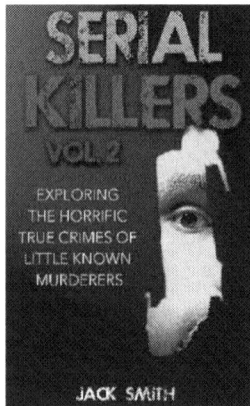
SERIAL KILLERS VOL 2 — EXPLORING THE HORRIFIC TRUE CRIMES OF LITTLE KNOWN MURDERERS — JACK SMITH

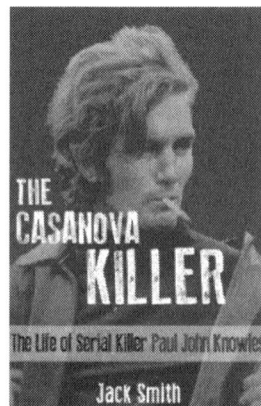
THE CASANOVA KILLER — The Life of Serial Killer Paul John Knowles — Jack Smith

Printed in Dunstable, United Kingdom